WILDLIFE VIEWING AREAS

Missouri Ecoregions

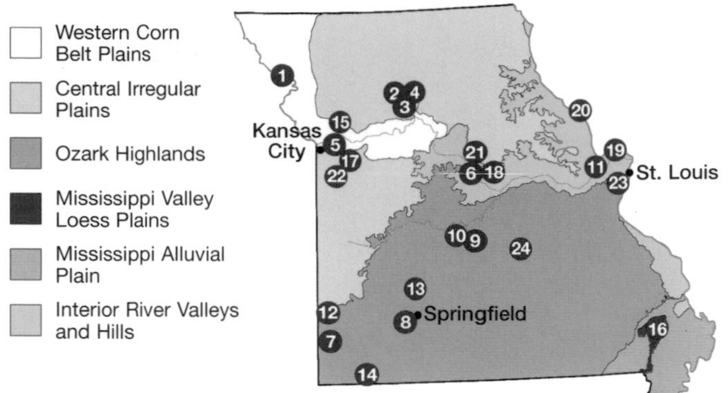

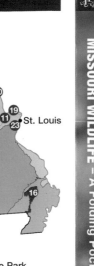

Western Corn Belt Plains
Central Irregular Plains
Ozark Highlands
Mississippi Valley Loess Plains
Mississippi Alluvial Plain
Interior River Valleys and Hills
Kansas City
St. Louis
Springfield

1. Squaw Creek National Wildlife Refuge
2. Fountain Grove Conservation Area
3. Swan Lake National Wildlife Refuge
4. Pershing State Park
5. Kansas City Museum
6. Eagle Bluffs Conservation Area
7. Wildcat Glades Conservation and Audubon Center
8. Springfield Conservation Nature Center
9. Lake of the Ozarks State Park
10. Ozark Caverns
11. Lewis & Clark Boat House and Nature Center
12. Prairie State Park
13. Bennett Spring State Park
14. Roaring River State Park
15. Martha LaFite Thompson Nature Sanctuary
16. Mingo National Wildlife Refuge
17. Burr Oak Woods Nature Center
18. Rock Bridge Memorial State Park
19. Audubon Center at Riverlands
20. Clarence Cannon National Wildlife Refuge
21. Big Muddy National Fish & Wildlife Refuge
22. Burroughs Audubon Nature Center and Sanctuary
23. St. Louis Science Center
24. Maramec Spring Park

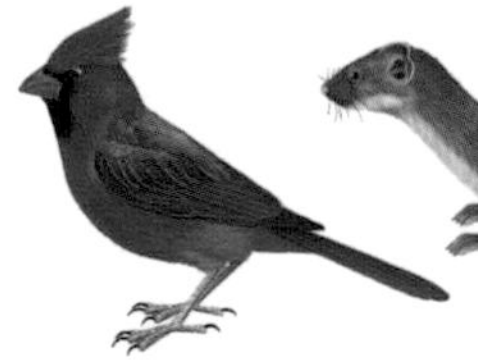

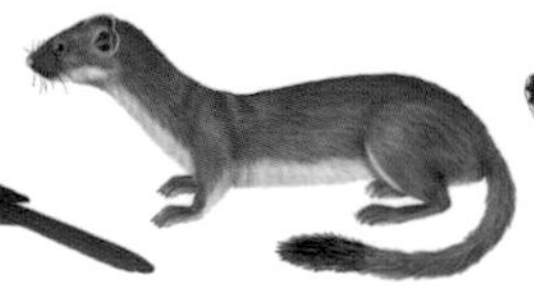

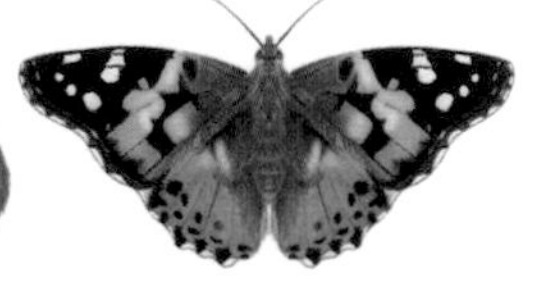

Most illustrations show the adult male in breeding coloration. Colors and markings may be duller or absent during different seasons. The measurements denote the length of species from nose/bill to tail tip. Butterfly measurements denote wingspan. Illustrations are not to scale.

Made in the USA

Waterford Press publishes reference guides that introduce readers to nature observation, outdoor recreation and survival skills. Product information is featured on the website: **www.waterfordpress.com**

To order or for information on custom published products please call 800-434-2555 or email orderdesk@waterfordpress.com. For permissions or to share comments email editor@waterfordpress.com.

ISBN 978-1-58355-594-1 $7.95 U.S.
9 781583 555941 50795
UPC 8 84682 01041 6
10 9 8 7 6 5 4 3 2 1 2301421

A POCKET NATURALIST® GUIDE

MISSOURI WILDLIFE

A Folding Pocket Guide to Familiar Animals

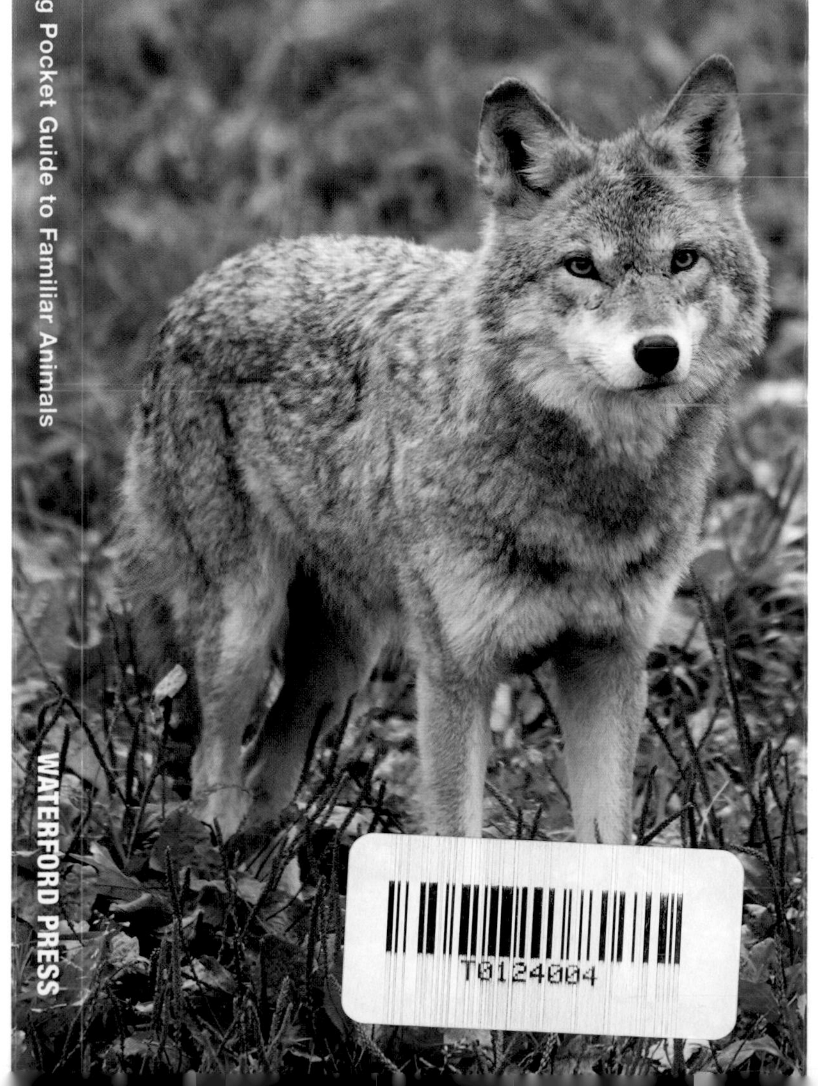

MISSOURI WILDLIFE – A Folding Pocket Guide to Familiar Animals

WATERFORD PRESS

T0124004

INVERTEBRATES

Field Cricket
Gryllus pennsylvanicus
To 1 in. (3 cm)
Shrill call is a series of 3 chirps.

True Katydid
Pterophylla camellifolia
To 2 in. (5 cm)
Loud 2-part call – *katy-DID* – is heard on summer evenings.

Cicada
Tibicen dorsata
To 1.5 in. (4 cm)
Song is a sudden loud whine or buzz, maintained steadily before dying away.

Crayfish
Family Cambaridae
To 5 in. (13 cm)
Missouri's state invertebrate.

Familiar Bluet
Enallagma civile
1.5 in. (4 cm)
A damselfly, it rests with its wings folded over its back.

Deer Tick
Dermacentor spp.
To .25 in. (.6 cm)
Feeds on the blood of mammals and can transmit disease-causing organisms between hosts.

Green Darner
Anax junius
To 3 in. (8 cm)
Like most dragonflies, it rests with its wings open.

Yellow Jacket
Vespula spp.
To .5 in. (1.3 cm)
Aggressive picnic pest can sting repeatedly.

Paper Wasp
Polistes spp.
To 1 in. (3 cm)
Builds papery hanging nests. Can sting repeatedly.

Honey Bee
Apis mellifera
To .75 in. (2 cm)
Slender bee has pollen baskets on its rear legs. Can only sting once.
Missouri's state insect.

Bumble Bee
Bombus spp.
To 1 in. (3 cm)
Stout, furry bee is large and noisy. Can sting repeatedly.

Firefly
Family Lampyridae
To .75 in. (2 cm)
Flashing, luminescent tail can be seen at night.

Black-and-yellow Garden Spider
Argiope aurantia
To 1.25 in. (3.2 cm)

Black Widow Spider
Latrodectus mactans
To .3 in. (8 mm)
Black spider is easily recognized by its shiny, bulbous abdomen with a red hourglass marking beneath. Venom can be lethal to children.

Chigger (Velvet Mite)
Family Trombidiidae
To .12 in. (.3 cm)
Tiny, biting woodland insects leave red welts on human skin.

Fiddleback Spider (Brown Recluse Spider)
Loxosceles reclusa
To .5 in. (1.5 cm)
Easily distinguished by its violin-shaped marking on its back. Bites cause tissue degeneration.

BUTTERFLIES

Eastern Tiger Swallowtail
Papilio glaucus
To 6 in. (15 cm)

Pipevine Swallowtail
Battus philenor
To 3.5 in. (9 cm)

Zebra Swallowtail
Eurytides marcellus
To 3.5 in. (9 cm)

Spicebush Swallowtail
Papilio troilus
To 4.5 in. (11 cm)

Cabbage White
Pieris rapae
To 2 in. (5 cm)
One of the most common butterflies.

Orange Sulphur
Colias eurytheme
To 2.5 in. (6 cm)

Painted Lady
Vanessa cardui
To 2.5 in. (6 cm)
Tip of forewing is dark with white spots.

Eastern Tailed Blue
Cupido comyntas
To 1 in. (3 cm)
Note orange spots above thread-like hindwing "tails."

Summer Azure
Celastrina neglecta
To 1 in. (3 cm)

Underwings

Silver-spotted Skipper
Epargyreus clarus
To 2.5 in. (6 cm)
Has a large, irregular silver patch on the underside of its hindwings.

Buckeye
Junonia coenia
To 2.5 in. (6 cm)

Monarch
Danaus plexippus
To 4 in. (10 cm)
Note rows of white spots on edges of wings.

Great Spangled Fritillary
Speyeria cybele
To 3 in. (8 cm)
Common in marshes and wet meadows.

American Snout
Libytheana carinenta
To 2 in. (5 cm)
"Snout" is formed from projecting mouth parts which enclose its coiled proboscis.

Underwings

Southern Pearly Eye
Enodia portlandia
To 2 in. (5 cm)
Note 4 spots on forewings and 6 spots on hindwings.

GAME FISHES

Rainbow Trout
Oncorhynchus mykiss To 44 in. (1.1 m)
Note reddish side stripe.

Brown Trout
Salmo trutta To 40 in. (1 m)

Bluegill
Lepomis macrochirus
To 16 in. (40 cm)

Gizzard Shad
Dorosoma cepedianum To 16 in. (41 cm)

Green Sunfish
Lepomis cyanellus To 12 in. (30 cm)
The most widely distributed fish in Missouri.

Paddlefish
Polyodon spathula To 7 ft. (2.1 m)
Has a long, paddle-shaped snout.
Missouri's state aquatic animal.

White Crappie
Pomoxis annularis To 20 in. (50 cm)

Largemouth Bass
Micropterus salmoides To 40 in. (1 m)
Jaw joint extends beyond the eye.

Flathead Catfish
Pylodictis olivaris To 5 ft. (1.5 m)
Head is long and flat. Upper lobe of caudal fin is white.

Smallmouth Bass
Micropterus dolomieu
To 27 in. (68 cm)
Jaw joint is beneath the eye.

Channel Catfish
Ictalurus punctatus To 4 ft. (1.2 m)
Missouri's state fish.

White Bass
Morone chrysops To 18 in. (45 cm)
Silvery fish has 4-7 dark side stripes.

Shovelnose Sturgeon
Scaphirhynchus platorynchus
To 3 ft. (90 cm)
Note upturned snout.

Rock Bass
Ambloplites rupestris To 17 in. (43 cm)
Note red eyes and side blotches.

Walleye
Sander vitreus To 40 in. (1 m)

REPTILES & AMPHIBIANS

American Toad
Anaxyrus americanus
To 4.5 in. (11 cm)
Call is a high musical trill lasting up to 30 seconds.

Green Frog
Lithobates clamitans
To 4 in. (10 cm)
Single-note call is a banjo-like twang.

Spring Peeper
Pseudacris crucifer
To 1.5 in. (4 cm)
Note dark X on back. Musical call is a series of short peeps.

Bullfrog
Lithobates catesbeianus
To 8 in. (20 cm)
Call is a deep-pitched – *jug-o-rum*.
Missouri's state amphibian.

Fence Lizard
Sceloporus undulatus
To 8 in. (20 cm)
Has dark, zigzag bars down its back.

Southern Leopard Frog
Rana utricularia
To 5 in. (13 cm)
Green to brown frog is covered with dark spots. Call is a series of short croaks.

Western Painted Turtle
Chrysemys picta bellii
To 10 in. (25 cm)

Snapping Turtle
Chelydra serpentina To 18 in. (45 cm)
Note knobby shell and long tail.

Three-toed Box Turtle
Terrapene carolina triunguis
To 8 in. (20 cm)
Missouri's state reptile.

Northern Water Snake
Nerodia sipedon To 4.5 ft. (1.4 m)
Note dark blotches on back.

Black Rat Snake
Elaphe obsoleta obsoleta
To 8 ft. (2.4 m)

Eastern Garter Snake
Thamnophis sirtalis sirtalis
To 4 ft. (1.2 m)

Copperhead
Agkistrodon contortrix To 52 in. (1.3 m)
Venomous snake has hourglass-shaped bands down its back.

Western Pigmy Rattlesnake
Sistrurus miliarius streckeri
To 31 in. (78 cm)
Venomous.

Cottonmouth
Agkistrodon piscivorus To 6 ft. (1.8 m)
Large, venomous water snake has a spade-shaped head.

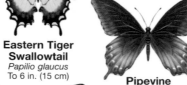

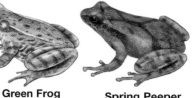

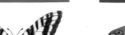

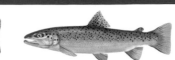

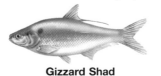

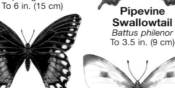

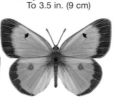

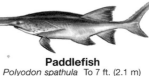

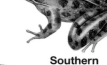

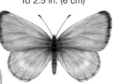

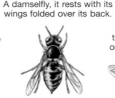

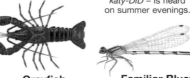

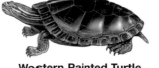

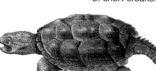

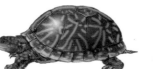

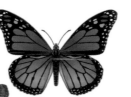

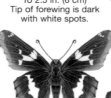

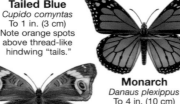

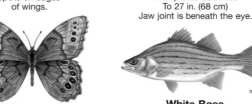

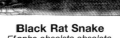

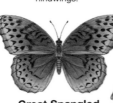

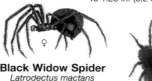

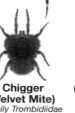

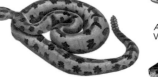

Mallard
Anas platyrhynchos To 28 in. (70 cm) ♂♀

Wood Duck
Aix sponsa To 20 in. (50 cm)

Green-winged Teal
Anas crecca To 16 in. (40 cm) ♂♀

Blue-winged Teal
Spatula discors To 16 in. (40 cm) ♀ ♂

Redhead
Aythya americana To 22 in. (55 cm) ♀

Common Merganser
Mergus merganser To 27 in. (68 cm) ♀ ♂

American Coot
Fulica americana To 16 in. (40 cm)

Green Heron
Butorides virescens To 22 in. (55 cm)

Snow Goose
Chen caerulescens To 31 in. (78 cm)

Great Blue Heron
Ardea herodias To 4.5 ft. (1.4 m)

Canada Goose
Branta canadensis To 45 in. (1.14 m)

Killdeer
Charadrius vociferus To 12 in. (30 cm)

Common Nighthawk
Chordeiles minor To 10 in. (25 cm) Often hawks for insects around street lights.

Mourning Dove
Zenaida macroura To 13 in. (33 cm) Call is a mournful – ooah-woo-woo-woo.

Rock Pigeon
Columba livia To 13 in. (33 cm)

Wild Turkey
Meleagris gallopavo To 4 ft. (1.2 m)

Northern Bobwhite
Colinus virginianus To 12 in. (30 cm) Missouri's state game bird.

Ruby-throated Hummingbird
Archilochus colubris To 3.5 in. (9 cm)

European Starling
Sturnus vulgaris To 8 in. (20 cm)

Ring-billed Gull
Larus delawarensis To 20 in. (50 cm) Bill has dark ring.

Downy Woodpecker
Dryobates pubescens To 6 in. (15 cm) The similar hairy woodpecker is larger and has a longer bill.

Belted Kingfisher
Megaceryle alcyon To 14 in. (35 cm)

Northern Flicker
Colaptes auratus To 13 in. (33 cm)

Red-bellied Woodpecker
Melanerpes carolinus To 11 in. (28 cm)

Turkey Vulture
Cathartes aura To 32 in. (80 cm)

Red-tailed Hawk
Buteo jamaicensis To 25 in. (63 cm)

Eastern Meadowlark
Sturnella magna To 9 in. (23 cm)

American Kestrel
Falco sparverius To 12 in. (30 cm)

Barred Owl
Strix varia To 2 ft. (60 cm) Call is a loud – who-cooks-for-you? who-cooks-for-you-all?

Great Horned Owl
Bubo virginianus To 25 in. (63 cm) Call is a resonant – hoo-HOO-hoooo.

Yellow-billed Cuckoo
Coccyzus americanus To 14 in. (35 cm)

Great Crested Flycatcher
Myiarchus crinitus To 9 in. (23 cm)

Tufted Titmouse
Baeolophus bicolor To 6 in. (15 cm)

White-breasted Nuthatch
Sitta carolinensis To 6 in. (15 cm)

Tree Swallow
Tachycineta bicolor To 6 in. (15 cm)

Barn Swallow
Hirundo rustica To 8 in. (20 cm) Note deeply forked tail.

Purple Martin
Progne subis To 8 in. (20 cm)

House Wren
Troglodytes aedon To 5 in. (13 cm)

Black-capped Chickadee
Poecile atricapillus To 6 in. (15 cm) Name-saying call is – chick-a-dee-dee-dee.

American Crow
Corvus brachyrhynchos To 22 in. (55 cm) Call is a distinct – caw.

Blue Jay
Cyanocitta cristata To 14 in. (35 cm)

Baltimore Oriole
Icterus galbula To 8 in. (20 cm)

Red-winged Blackbird
Agelaius phoeniceus To 9 in. (23 cm) Song is a gurgling – konk-la-reee – followed by a trill.

Common Grackle
Quiscalus quiscula To 14 in. (35 cm)

Brown Thrasher
Toxostoma rufum To 12 in. (30 cm)

Eastern Bluebird
Sialia sialis To 7 in. (18 cm) Missouri's state bird.

American Robin
Turdus migratorius To 11 in. (28 cm)

Northern Mockingbird
Mimus polyglottos To 11 in. (28 cm)

Dark-eyed Junco
Junco hyemalis To 7 in. (18 cm)

Gray Catbird
Dumetella carolinensis To 9 in. (23 cm) Note black cap. Call has cat-like *mew* notes.

Indigo Bunting
Passerina cyanea To 6 in. (15 cm)

Common Yellowthroat
Geothlypis trichas To 7 in. (18 cm)

Yellow-rumped Warbler
Setophaga coronata To 6 in. (15 cm)

Cedar Waxwing
Bombycilla cedrorum To 7 in. (18 cm) Red wing marks look like waxy droplets.

Song Sparrow
Melospiza melodia To 7 in. (18 cm) Note central breast spot.

House Sparrow
Passer domesticus To 6 in. (15 cm)

American Goldfinch
Spinus tristis To 5 in. (13 cm)

Eastern Towhee
Pipilo erythrophthalmus To 9 in. (23 cm) Cheerful song is – drink-your-tea or drink-tea.

Blue Grosbeak
Passerina caerulea To 8 in. (20 cm)

Summer Tanager
Piranga rubra To 8 in. (20 cm)

Northern Cardinal
Cardinalis cardinalis To 9 in. (23 cm)

Virginia Opossum
Didelphis virginiana To 40 in. (1 m) Note long fur and naked tail.

Tri-colored
Perimyotis subflavus To 3.5 in. (9 cm) The most common Missouri cave bat.

Big Brown Bat
Eptesicus fuscus To 5 in. (13 cm)

Fox Squirrel
Sciurus niger To 28 in. (70 cm) Note large size and bushy tail. Largest squirrel in the US.

Southern Flying Squirrel
Glaucomys volans To 10 in. (25 cm)

Eastern Gray Squirrel
Sciurus carolinensis To 20 in. (50 cm)

Woodchuck
Marmota monax To 32 in. (80 cm) Also called a groundhog.

Nine-banded Armadillo
Dasypus novemcinctus To 32 in. (80 cm)

Deer Mouse
Peromyscus maniculatus To 8 in. (20 cm)

Eastern Cottontail
Sylvilagus floridanus To 18 in. (45 cm)

Norway Rat
Rattus norvegicus To 18 in. (45 cm) Brown to gray rodent has a naked tail.

Muskrat
Ondatra zibethicus To 2 ft. (60 cm) Aquatic rodent has a naked tail that is flattened on its sides.

American Beaver
Castor canadensis To 4 ft. (1.2 m)

American Badger
Taxidea taxus To 35 in. (88 cm)

Striped Skunk
Mephitis mephitis To 32 in. (80 cm)

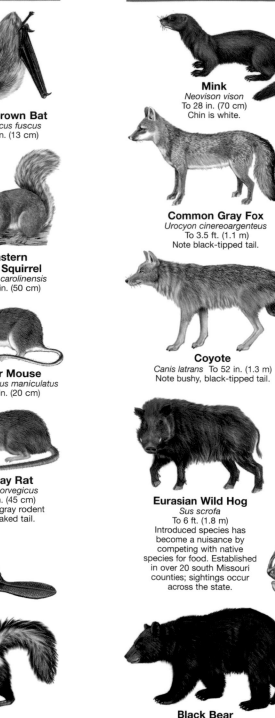

Mink
Neovison vison To 28 in. (70 cm) Chin is white.

Long-tailed Weasel
Mustela frenata To 21 in. (53 cm) Note brown feet and yellowish neck.

Common Gray Fox
Urocyon cinereoargenteus To 3.5 ft. (1.1 m) Note black-tipped tail.

Northern River Otter
Lontra canadensis To 52 in. (1.3 m)

Coyote
Canis latrans To 52 in. (1.3 m) Note bushy, black-tipped tail.

Red Fox
Vulpes vulpes To 40 in. (1 m) Note white-tipped tail.

Common Raccoon
Procyon lotor To 40 in. (1 m)

Eurasian Wild Hog
Sus scrofa To 6 ft. (1.8 m) Introduced species has become a nuisance by competing with native species for food. Established in over 20 south Missouri counties; sightings occur across the state.

Bobcat
Lynx rufus To 4 ft. (1.2 m)

Black Bear
Ursus americanus To 6 ft. (1.8 m)

White-tailed Deer
Odocoileus virginianus To 7 ft. (2.1 m)